127 HOURS

ARON RALSTON

Adapted from *Between a rock and a hard place*
by Aron Ralston

HELBLING

Adapted by: Rodney Smith

Publisher: Jacquie Bloese

Editor: Patricia Reilly

Designer: Ellipsis Digital Ltd

Picture research: Pupak Navabpour

Photo credits:
Page 4: W Skrypczak/Alamy.
Page 6: Aurora Photos, LOOK Die Bildagentur der Fotografen GmbH/ Alamy; J Jurica, K Schoen/iStockphoto.
Page 9: W Skrypczak/Alamy.
Page 22: M Konrad/iStockphoto.
Page 24: D Cardiff/iStockphoto.
Page 27: Juniors Bildarchiv/Alamy.
Page 32: Marmaduke St. John/Alamy.
Page 39: Photonica/Getty Images.
Page 40: julichka/iStockphoto.
Page 43: E Westmacott/Alamy.
Pages 56 & 57: Twentieth Century Fox Film Corporation; I Gavan/Getty Images; Photos 12/Alamy.
Pages 58 & 59: appleuzr, J Margolis, P Evans/iStockphoto; C Selby, Aurora Photos/Alamy.
Pages 60 & 61: M Ralston/AFP/Getty Images; M Sayle, N Ulevich/PA Photos.

Published by Scholastic Ltd. 2012

Mary Glasgow Magazines (Scholastic Ltd.)
Euston House
24 Eversholt Street
London NW1 1DB

Printed in Malaysia. Reprinted in 2013, 2014, 2015, 2016, 2017 and 2018.

Contents

Contents	Page
127 Hours	**4–55**
People and places	**4**
Canyons and canyoning	**6**
Prologue	**8**
Chapter 1: 'The most beautiful place on Earth'	**9**
Chapter 2: The accident	**14**
Chapter 3: Three plans	**18**
Chapter 4: Night and day	**21**
Chapter 5: A sad message	**24**
Chapter 6: Waiting	**27**
Chapter 7: 'Where's Aron?'	**31**
Chapter 8: The raven	**35**
Chapter 9: 'It's his truck'	**41**
Chapter 10: Escape	**44**
Chapter 11: 127 hours	**50**
Epilogue	**53**
Fact Files	**56–61**
Making *127 Hours*	**56**
Utah, a land of parks and canyons	**58**
'Anything is possible': disability and sports	**60**
Self-Study Activities	**62–64**
New Words	**inside back cover**

ARON RALSTON

Aron Ralston is a mountain climber from Colorado, USA. In April 2003, he went to Canyonlands National Park in Utah to hike the Horseshoe Canyon Trail. On April the 26th, Aron had planned a day of biking and hiking, but he had a terrible accident. This is his story.

PLACES

CANYONLANDS

Canyonlands is the biggest National Park in Utah, USA It is a beautiful tourist area of yellow and orange rock, deep canyons and tall mountains. Hiking, mountain-climbing, canyoning and biking are all popular here. Moab is the closest main town.

THE HORSESHOE TRAIL

This trail, with different hikes, is a part of Canyonlands National Park. The most popular part of the trail is about eight kilometres long. Aron goes on a difficult hike.

MAP KEY

1 Aron leaves his truck.
2 Aron leaves his bike and starts his hike.
3 Aron meets Kristi and Megan.
4 Megan and Kristi say goodbye.
5 The difficult part of the trail begins.
6 The accident – Aron's arm is trapped by a boulder.
7 Aron arrives at the Big Drop Rappel.
8 Aron meets the Dutch family.
9 The helicopter arrives.

Aron's journey

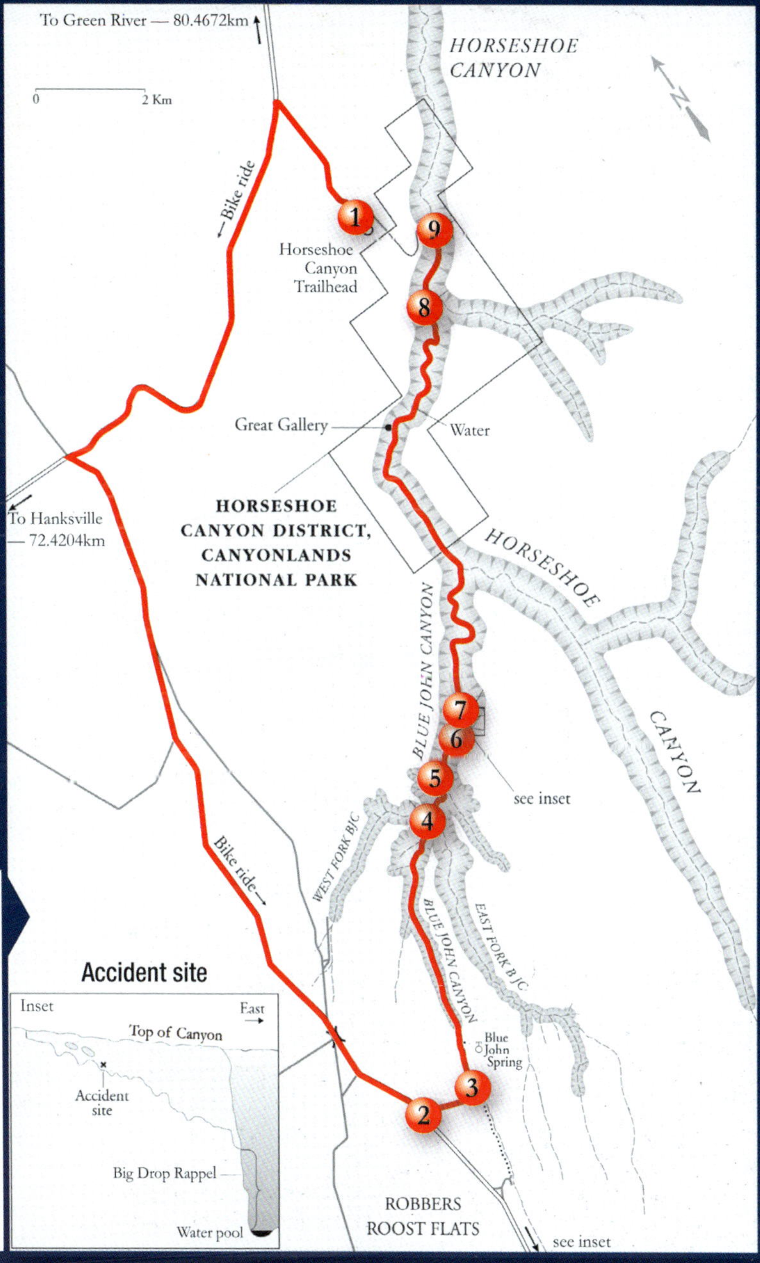

Canyons and canyoning

A **canyon** is a long, deep valley with very steep sides. Canyons are usually made of rock, but in cold places there are also ice canyons. **Canyoning** is travelling through canyons by walking, climbing, swimming or jumping.

Rappelling means using a rope to go down a very steep rock. The place where this happens can also be called a **rappel**, or a **drop**. Aron manages to rappel with one arm after his accident!

Chimneying is a way of climbing in narrow spaces using your back, arms, and legs. It is important to be able to **chimney** to travel through canyons. Aron was chimneying when he had his accident.

Boulders are very large rocks. Sometimes, heavy rain can carry them to narrow canyons where they get stuck between the walls. Here, they are dangerous because they can move or even fall.

CANYONING EQUIPMENT

This is the equipment that Aron took on his trip. He also took a camcorder and a digital camera.

127 HOURS

PROLOGUE

You are going to die.

I hear the voice in my head. I call it my first voice. It always comes after I've made some kind of mistake. Its words never help, they just make me feel bad. So I wait for the second voice. Its words are calm and sensible and nearly always help me. I wait, but tonight the second voice doesn't come. There is only silence, darkness and cold.

In the first days, the second voice always came. It stopped me feeling sad, angry, or afraid. It gave me ideas. It showed me things. It brought me hope. I believed I could be free again. But, slowly, that voice disappeared. My belief disappeared with it. Now there is only the first voice. It says the same thing over and over again. Finally, I must accept the truth: I am going to die.

CHAPTER 1
'The most beautiful place on Earth'

It is Saturday, April the 26th, 2003. My name is Aron Ralston. I'm biking and hiking in Canyonlands National Park in south-east Utah, USA. Edward Abbey, one of my favourite writers, described it as 'the most beautiful place on Earth'. Right now, with the sun on my back and the wind in my hair, I agree.

Today is the third day of an activity holiday. It started on Thursday when I went climbing and skiing on Mount Soplis with my friend, Brad. Yesterday, I biked the Slick Rock Trail, alone. It's not very long – only a little over nineteen kilometres – but it's one of the most difficult bike trails in the US. Today, my plan is to hike through Blue John and Horseshoe Canyons after biking to the trail. I'll leave my bike at the end of the trail and hike back to the carpark. I'll drive over in the truck and collect the bike later.

After that, I'll drive to Goblin Valley, about eighty kilometres north of here. My friends are having a party there. I hope I get some sleep because tomorrow I want to hike the most popular trail in southern Utah – Little White Horse.

I plan to spend the whole of Monday biking along the White Rim Trail. The trail forms a rough circle of 175 kilometres. It's not difficult and I should be able to finish in about eighteen hours. By Monday evening, I'll be back in Aspen, Colorado. Aspen is famous for its mountains and the countryside around it. It's a popular place for skiing. I live there and I work for Ute Mountaineer, a sports equipment shop. Leona, one of the people I live and work with, is having a goodbye party on Monday night. Now that winter is over, she's going to another town in Colorado to work as a gardener for the summer. Her party will be a cool way to end my trip.

* * *

00 hrs

8.45 am I arrive at the Horseshoe Canyon carpark* early in the morning, pull my bike from the truck and lock the door. Then I check the time: eight forty-five in the morning. As I start cycling, I wonder how quickly I can get to the start of the trail.

I can now see the sign pointing to this end of the trail. That means I've cycled thirteen kilometres in less than two hours. That's good. It will give me more time to finish my hike back to the truck. I lock my bike to a tree and start walking.

As I walk, I think about the history of the people who were here before me. One of them, Butch Cassidy, was

* See the map in People and places, pages 4-5.

very famous. He and his men stole horses and hid from the law during the last years of the nineteenth century. Since that time, the area has been called Robbers Roost country.

My climbing bag is heavy with the weight of my equipment. I think about my plan for the day. Blue John Canyon will be the most difficult part of the hike. Three kilometres along the trail is the Big Drop Rappel. Here, the canyon suddenly drops eighteen metres. The hardest part is 180 metres before this. The walls there are very narrow and the trail goes up and down, sharply. There are also a lot of very large rocks called boulders, stuck between the canyon walls. If these boulders move or fall they can be dangerous.

But I'm not thinking of danger at the moment. I am excited. Today, I will finally see the Great Gallery. The Gallery is part of Horseshoe Canyon, and it's famous for the huge rock paintings which cover its walls. Some of them are more than five thousand years old. I should reach my truck by late afternoon. So far, things are going well. I arrived here earlier than I thought. This gives me a little more time to finish my trip.

I always get very excited when I'm about to leave on a trip. This means I sometimes forget things. Before starting this trip, I forgot to leave a message telling anyone exactly where I was going. This is one of the things my mother taught me. But this time, I just called a quick goodbye to my housemates – Brian, Joe, and Leona. Leona asked where I was going. I told her I was going to Utah and promised to be back for her party. Then I got in my truck and drove away. I can't wait for adventure. It makes me feel happier than anything. It's part of who I am.

* * *

I'm on a high rock, looking down at the trail. I've stopped because I can hear voices. This surprises me. I had expected to be alone. Two young women suddenly appear below me. I feel pleased. I've spent the last eighteen hours alone. It will be good to have company for a while.

'Hi,' I call as I climb down the rock. The girls hadn't noticed me. They turn, looking a little nervous. I guess they are about twenty-five years old.

I smile and hold out my hand, 'My name's Aron.'

They smile back. 'I'm Megan,' says the darker girl, 'and this is Kristi.'

We shake hands and continue along the trail. As we go, we talk about our interests. We all love hiking, biking and adventures. For all of us, this is more important than earning a lot of money. They work in the same business, too. They work for Outward Bound, a sports equipment shop in Moab,

Utah. Both Aspen and Moab are important tourist centres for hikers.

We are on the trail together for about five kilometres. At that point, there is a smaller canyon to the west. The west canyon goes back in a half-circle. The girls left their bikes at the end of it. We will say goodbye there and I'll continue on alone to the Big Drop Rappel.

We arrive just before 2.00 pm. I don't feel like saying goodbye. In the hour and a half we've been together, we've already become friends.

Megan feels the same. 'Why don't you come with us?' she asks. 'We can finish the west canyon trail, go back to our truck and have a few beers.'

I like the idea, but following my plan is more important. I ask them to come with me.

'How far is it back to your truck?' Megan asks.

'Around thirteen kilometres.'

'That's too far. You won't get back before dark,' she says.

'Maybe not, but I really want to do the Big Drop Rappel. And I can't miss the paintings in the Great Gallery. I'll meet you after for a drink.'

We agree on a plan to meet and go to the party together.

Then I turn and wave goodbye. The movement is so easy I don't think about it. But there is something I don't know. It is the last time I will wave goodbye with my right hand.

CHAPTER 2
The accident

The girls disappear into the west canyon. I am alone again. I continue walking towards the Big Drop Rappel. It seems strangely quiet without Kristi and Megan. I turn on my CD player and listen to a soft, slow song by Phish, one of my favourite bands.

The music is perfect for the way I feel: lucky, free and happy. The weather is perfect, too. It's warm and sunny with just a few white clouds in the sky.

Suddenly, my feet hit a pile of loose stones and I nearly fall to the ground.

Careful, Aron.

I listen to the voice in my head and look up the canyon. I can see that the trail ahead becomes more difficult. The Big Drop Rappel is now just under a kilometre away.

Twenty minutes later, I arrive at the most difficult part

of the trail. Here, the canyon walls are a lot narrower. The trail rises and falls and is full of sharp rocks. I will have to be careful. I look up and see part of a tree stuck between the canyon walls. It was carried along the canyon after heavy rain. This is one of the dangers of hiking in canyon country. After a sudden storm, canyons can quickly fill with water. In seconds, the water can throw you against the canyon walls and kill you. That's why it's always very important to check the weather before canyoning.

Just below the tree is the first drop in the trail. It's only about three metres, so I won't need any equipment. There are plenty of holes in the rock for my hands and feet so I climb down easily. A metre from the bottom I let go and land on the ground. Soft sand covers the tops of my boots. From here it would be difficult to climb back up. One thing is immediately clear: I can't go back.

* * *

The canyon walls become even narrower. Stuck between them, as far as I can see, are boulders of different sizes. It's an unusual sight. I stop and take a few pictures with my camera.

The Big Drop Rappel is now only about 160 metres away. Climbing down will be no problem. I have all the equipment I need in my backpack. For food, I have two burritos*. I also have a full water bottle and an extra two litres in a CamelBak.

The boulders are both good and bad news. The good news is that I should be able to climb over many of them. This will be quicker than dropping on to the trail and climbing back up again. The bad news is that the boulders could move. I will have to be careful.

I manage the first few boulders without any problems and reach another drop. This one is about four metres down. About three metres from the edge of the drop is a boulder. It's about the same size as the wheel of a bus. If I climb onto it, the drop from there will be shorter. I chimney** to the boulder quite easily.

As I stand on it, I feel something move. The movement stops almost immediately. It seems there's nothing to worry about. I lie down, put my hands in two holes on the far edge of the boulder and push my legs over the opposite side to jump down.

As most of my weight pushes on one side of the boulder, it makes a strange sound. Immediately I know this is trouble but it's too late to go back. From this point, everything seems to happen very slowly. I let go of the boulder and drop towards the ground. As I fall, I look up and see the boulder crashing towards my head. If I don't get out of the way, I'm dead. I try to push against the boulder with both hands. It hits my left hand hard against the canyon wall. I pull it back with a scream of pain. The boulder then hits my right arm and traps my hand against the right side of the canyon.

* A burrito is like a sandwich. It comes from Mexico.

** See Canyons and canyoning, page 6.

6 hrs

2.45 pm All this happens in a couple of seconds. I don't even notice landing on the canyon floor. I am so shocked I feel no pain. I just stand there, looking at my trapped hand in disbelief.

Stupid, Aron, stupid! When you first stood on the rock it moved. That was a clear message to stay away! But you were in such a hurry to finish the hike you didn't stop and check.

The voice in my head doesn't help. It just makes things worse.

A terrible pain travels up my arm. I scream and pull hard to try and free myself. Nothing happens. I try again. This time I push against the boulder with my knees at the same time.

It's no good. The boulder is a lot heavier than I am.

I am stuck and there's no way out.

CHAPTER 3
Three plans

Stop thinking about how bad the problem is, Aron. You need to be sensible.

The voice in my head is right. I must be sensible. This has to be my rule from now on.

The first thing I need is a drink. Without stopping to think, I take the water bottle from my bag and drink a third of it in five seconds.

I suddenly realise what I'm doing and pull the bottle out of my mouth. Already, I have broken my rule to be sensible. I have no idea how long I will be here. This means that the most important thing of all is to save water.

Damn it, Aron! Stupid! Stupid! Stupid!

* * *

6 hrs 43 mins

3.28 pm It's almost forty-five minutes since my accident. I am calmer than before. For the last half hour I've been thinking of my best chance of escape. I said I would meet Kristi and Megan after the hike. If I don't appear, will they go to my truck to find me? I won't be there. But will they realise that something is wrong and go for help?

The answer is probably 'no'. Kristi and Megan don't know me very well. They'll just think that I decided not to meet them. What about other hikers? Will they find me by chance? Again, the answer is probably 'no'. Very few people travel to the Great Gallery from this end of the trail. My friends won't worry, either. They weren't completely sure I was going to the party. Even on Monday evening, my housemates will just think I'm late getting back. No one will miss me until Tuesday morning. When I don't arrive for work, Brion After, my boss, will know that something is wrong. I am never late for work. He will probably call my family and they will tell the police that I am missing. But I didn't tell anyone exactly where I was going, so it will take the police days to find me. If I don't escape before then, I will die.

All of this means that I will have to get out of here alone. But how?

I can think of three possible plans. The first plan is to use the large knife on the multi-tool to chip at the boulder. This might take away enough of the rock to free my hand. The second plan is to try and lift the boulder using some of my equipment. The third plan is the worst. I could amputate my arm using the multi-tool. It's too soon to think of that idea.

I try plan one. I take the multi-tool from my climbing bag. It has two knives. One is longer than the other. I use the longest one which is not so sharp. To free my hand, I must remove a piece of rock over fifteen centimetres wide and seven centimetres deep. That's a lot of rock.

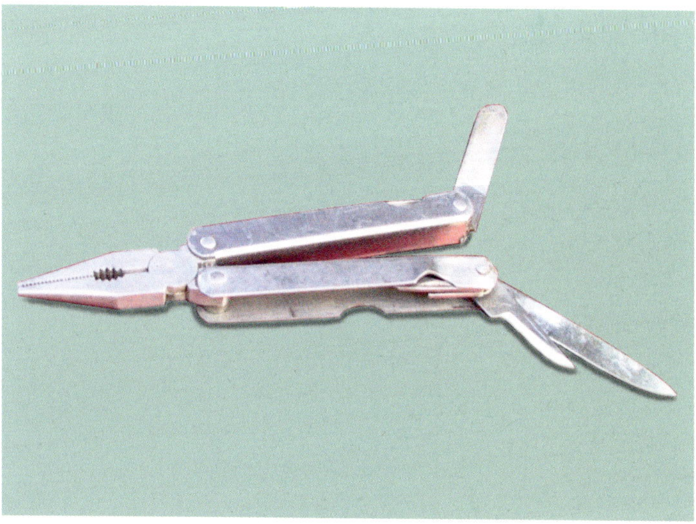

10 hrs 15 mins

7.00 pm I've been chipping at the rock for almost three and a half hours. I stop for a drink of water. I lay the multi-tool on the boulder and reach for the water bottle. This time I am more careful and take only a sip. I wonder how long I'll be able to survive with the water I have left, only two-thirds of a litre. Until Monday night, maybe? Tuesday morning at the latest.

CHAPTER 4
Night and day

After Kristi and Megan left Aron, they got lost in the west canyon and arrived late at the meeting place. He wasn't there.

'He's probably left already,' said Megan, 'but he can't be far away. Let's drive around and see if we can find him.'

But there was no sign of Aron or his bike. 'It doesn't really matter,' said Megan. 'We'll see him at the party.'

Again, she was wrong. By the time they reached Goblin Valley, the car park was full and there was nowhere to stay for the night.

The girls now felt very tired and decided not to go to the party. 'We'll drive to Little Wild Horse Canyon tomorrow morning,' said Megan. 'We'll probably find Aron there.'

Kristi agreed and they parked by the side of the road for the night.

The next morning, there was no sign of Aron at Little Wild Horse Canyon. All they found was a truck from Colorado with a bike inside and skis on the roof.

'That's probably Aron's truck,' said Megan. 'He must be in the canyon already. We've missed him again.'

She wrote their email addresses on a piece of paper and left it on the truck window.

'Why didn't we just get his phone number?' Megan asked as they drove back to Moab.

* * *

⌛ 15 hrs 15 mins

12.00 am My headlamp is on and I'm chipping at the boulder. I've managed to chip a space above and below an area of pink rock. Perhaps I can remove this large piece before I stop for the night. I will need to hit it hard. I don't want to break the knife, so I use a different part of the multi-tool. I hit the boulder as hard as I can and the piece of rock falls onto my trapped arm. I can now see some softer rock below. I chip at the rock for another hour and remove as much as the piece that came off before. More success, but my left arm hurts and I have to stop.

I take a sip of water. I have decided to do this every ninety minutes. I look up at the sky. It's a clear night and it's very cold.

Now that I've stopped chipping I feel cold. The wind is the worst. Every few minutes, it blows down the canyon and makes my body shake. I decide to use my climbing bag as a jacket to keep warm. I lay everything inside it on top of the boulder. Then I put the bag back on. I'm a little warmer but I need something soft to put my legs on. I take my rope, form it into a circle, and lay it on a rock below me. Now I can rest my knees instead of standing up all the time.

After a while, I begin to feel uncomfortable again. The problem is the weight on my legs. I decide to try and build some kind of seat. I put on my harness and rope. Then I tie carabiners to one end of the rope and make a kind of ball. The idea is to throw the rope over one of the boulders above my head. If I do it right, the ball will stick in the space between the boulder and the canyon wall.

It takes twenty-five throws before it lands in the right place. Now, will it hold my weight? I sit in the harness. It holds. Success! I feel very happy. But I'm not comfortable for long. I soon need to move again. I stand and chip for twenty minutes, then sit and rest for twenty minutes. This becomes my routine.

As morning comes, I'm not feeling too unhappy. This first night was not as bad as I thought. I've done quite well, but one thought still worries me: I haven't chipped much rock from the boulder. At this speed, it will take me 150 hours to free my trapped arm.

Chipping is not enough. I will have to think of something else.

CHAPTER 5
A sad message

23 hrs 30 mins

8.15 am I am feeling optimistic. The sun is shining into the canyon and a raven has just flown across the blue sky above my head. The sight and sound of the bird fills me with hope.

I hold my leg in the sunlight. It feels warm against my skin. But I need to do something. It's time for plan two. I will use my ropes, webbing and carabiners to try and lift the boulder and free my hand. I look up. There's a sharp piece of rock above my head. If I can throw the rope around this, it might hold everything in the right position.

After many tries, I finally succeed. I tie the other end of the rope around the boulder. But when I pull, nothing happens. Everything holds, but the boulder doesn't move. I put more weight on the rope, but it still doesn't work. The rope is not tight enough.

28 hrs 15 mins

1.00 pm I've spent four hours trying to lift the boulder, but nothing has worked.

Suddenly, I hear voices.

'Help! Help!' I shout.

I stop and listen. At first, there's nothing. But then I hear a sound from above and realise my mistake. It's just a small animal moving in the rock. I'd imagined it was people.

The sound of my voice shouting for help frightened me. It made me feel lost and alone. I make a promise that I won't do it again. The optimistic feelings of earlier in the day have disappeared. No one is going to save me. That leaves only the third, and worst, plan: I will have to amputate my right arm. What will I need for the job? The knife, that's certain, but also a tourniquet to stop the blood. The plastic pipe from the CamelBak seems best for that. I take it off and use a carabiner to make it tight. It works well and I feel a bit better.

As soon as I put the knife against the skin of my arm, I feel ill. I can't do it. It would be like killing myself. I drop the knife and lay my head on the boulder. None of my plans have worked. I can't free my hand. I can't lift the boulder. I can't amputate my arm. My only hope is rescue, but I'll die before help arrives.

I feel angry with the boulder, but it's not the boulder's fault – it's mine. Everything about this stupid adventure was a mistake. I didn't tell anyone where I was going, I didn't go with Kristi and Megan to the west canyon, and I didn't get off the boulder when it moved.

30 hrs

2.45 pm It's exactly twenty-four hours since the accident. I decide it's time to film a message for my family and friends. I place my camcorder on the boulder, turn it on and start speaking.

'My name is Aron Ralston. It's just after three o'clock on Sunday, April the 27th, 2003. I have been trapped in Blue John Canyon for the last twenty-four hours. My parents are Donna and Larry Ralston of Eaglewood, Colorado. If anyone finds this, please give it to them. Thank you.'

I describe all that has happened in the last two days. As I reach the end of my story I feel very sad. I know this could be a final goodbye to my parents and sister, Sonja.

After telling them how much I love them, there is only one more thing to say. 'Mum, Dad, Sonja – I'm sorry.'

I turn off the machine. All I can do now is wait for someone to find me.

CHAPTER 6
Waiting

33 hrs 15 mins

6.00 pm My second night in the canyon is moving closer. Beyond that, I see no future. Escape has been impossible and I will die before anyone finds me. I feel strong enough to survive the fear of death, but not my body's need for water. This terrible, growing thirst will drive me crazy.

I now have only a quarter of a litre of water left. I have to make this last as long as possible. I drank at 3.15 pm, just after I finished filming. Then I missed the next drink and decided to save it for later. I'll drink at nine, midnight, three and six in the morning, but I'll take even smaller sips.

The mosquitoes have found me. There are several at my feet and some drinking the blood on the canyon wall. I kill five or six as they circle around my head. Can I eat them, I wonder? Even if I could, it wouldn't be enough to keep me alive.

I go back to waiting. It seems colder than the night before. I start chipping at the boulder just to keep warm.

36 hrs 15 mins

9.00 pm Night has fallen. The mosquitoes have gone. The sky above is beautiful: clear with bright stars. But clear skies mean lower temperatures. I must do something to cover more of my body.

I tie the camera bag around my left arm. Then I tie webbing around my right arm and put rope around each of my legs. I do the same for my right arm, using webbing. I put rope round each leg. It looks funny and I can't help smiling.

I begin my routine of standing and sitting. Most of my body feels warmer, but I'm still shaking because my head and neck are cold. I decide to put the plastic rope bag over my head. I keep the far end open to let fresh air in. I lay my head against the boulder. I still can't sleep but at least I'm warmer.

The long, boring hours of the night pass slowly by. Finally, the sky grows lighter. Today, it's a dirty white colour. I wonder if this is cloud. Clouds at night are good because they trap the day's heat in the canyon, but clouds during the day are bad because the sun doesn't warm the air. There's also the chance of a storm.

Slowly the pale sky turns bright blue. It's going to be hot again. As always, the light and warm air make me want to do something. I try and lift the boulder again by pushing down on the rope with my feet.

This doesn't work either and I feel suddenly hopeless. What more can I do? No voice inside my head suggests anything useful. All I see in my mind are pictures of the food and drink left on the floor of my truck.

I think again about amputating my arm. I didn't try hard enough the last time. I need to be brave and try again.

I put on the tourniquet and make it tight. When everything is ready, I try to cut through the skin of my arm with the longer knife. I push hard but the skin doesn't break. Then, over the same area, I use the shorter, sharper knife. But even that doesn't work. It's still not sharp enough to do the job. All I have for the time I've spent on this is a long red line across my right arm. I take off the tourniquet and go back to waiting.

* * *

47 hrs 30 mins

8.15 am The raven appears. I check my watch. It has arrived at exactly the same time as yesterday.

For the first time in two days, I need to urinate. I open my shorts and watch the yellow urine disappear into the sand.

I spend most of the day chipping, resting, and counting the minutes before my next drink of water.

54 hrs

2.45 pm It's the middle of the afternoon and time to film again. Filming has now become a part of my daily routine. I turn on the camcorder.

'Hi, everyone. It's Monday, April the 28th. I'm still trapped. I've been here for exactly forty-eight hours. That's two whole days with no sleep and very little water. I now have only about one-eighth of a litre left.'

I continue with a message to my sister, Sonja. She is getting married in the autumn. I tell her how proud I am of her and send her my love and best wishes.

I finish filming at 3.35 pm. It's strange but I feel the need to urinate again. This time, my second voice tells me not to urinate on the ground.

Save it, Aron. It will soon be all you have to drink.

It's good advice. I urinate into the CamelBak. The urine is now a dark orange colour. The other urine was clearer. Why didn't I save it?

* * *

57 hrs 15 mins

6.00 pm It's early evening. Sunlight shines off the bottom of thin clouds high above me. I hope they will stay and keep the heat in the canyon. But as time passes, it seems to grow colder. My water won't last much longer. Soon, I will have to start drinking urine.

Like the raven, the mosquitoes seem to arrive on time. I kill a few more. Mosquitoes mean there must be water quite close – probably at the Big Drop Rappel.

Forget it, Aron. You'll never see water again.

The first voice is back. I try not to listen.

CHAPTER 7
'Where's Aron?'

Back in Aspen, Aron's housemates were preparing for the party. Elliot, another friend of his, was moving into the house after Leona had gone. At eight-thirty, he asked, 'Has anyone seen Aron?'

'No,' said Brian. 'He's probably still on his trip.'

'Does he know about the party?' Elliot asked.

'Of course,' said Leona. 'He said he'd be here for sure. He'd better come. It's my goodbye party. I'll be upset if he doesn't come.'

The party ended at around two o'clock the next morning, but there was still no sign of Aron.

The first person to think something might be wrong was Aron's boss, Brion. Early Tuesday morning, he called the house and spoke to Leona.

'He didn't come to the party last night,' Leona told him. 'I thought he'd driven straight to work.'

'No, he's not here, and Aron's never late. I think something might be wrong. Could you call me right away if he gets back?'

'Yes, sure,' said Leona, feeling a little worried.

She called Brion later that afternoon to ask if Aron had arrived.

'No,' said Brion. 'Did he say where he was going?'

'He didn't say much to any of us. Only that he was going climbing and biking. He also said he might hike in Utah. Somewhere in Canyonlands. He didn't say where, exactly.'

'Mmm, that's a big area,' said Brion. 'I'll wait until nine o'clock tomorrow morning. If he's not back by then, I'll call his parents.'

A police officer works on a search and rescue operation.

Aron's housemates decided not to wait any longer. At six-thirty that evening, they called the police. The officer on the desk asked for Aron's information: full name, age, height and weight. He also wanted to know the model of his truck and the license-plate number. But there was something the officer didn't tell them: a person has to be missing for at least forty-eight hours before the police will start a search and rescue operation. This meant that they wouldn't do anything until late the following day.

* * *

63 hrs 15 mins

12.00 am It's my third night here and I've decided to take my first sip of urine. There's still half a cup of water left, but I want to save it.

The urine tastes bad, but not quite as bad as I thought. I decide not to drink any more until the water is finished. I've changed my drinking routine because the night is colder. I can now only sit for a few minutes so I take smaller sips every hour.

66 hrs 15 mins

3.00 am It's now sixty hours since my accident. That's sixty hours of pain, no sleep, and very little water.

Two hours later, it's time for my next sip of water. I put the bottle between my legs and turn the top. When it's open, I try and lift it towards my mouth. But it hits my harness and falls back onto my legs. I am too tired to catch it. Some of the valuable water falls onto my shorts.

'Damn! Damn! Damn!' I shout.

Now look what you've done! says the first voice.

I know exactly what I've done. I've just lost half of the rest of my life.

70 hrs

6.45 am As morning arrives once more, I feel a little hope. At least I've survived another night. It's now Tuesday, April the 29th: my fourth day trapped in the canyon.

I decide to film earlier today. I put the camcorder on the boulder, then turn the screen the other way. I don't want to look at myself as I speak.

'Hi. It's Tuesday morning. I guess everyone missed me when I didn't arrive for Leona's party last night. Most people will probably think I'm still travelling. Except for Brion. When I don't arrive for work, he'll think something is wrong. He might call the police and report me missing. They'll wait forty-eight hours before searching. If I'm lucky, they'll start some time on Wednesday. If I'm very lucky, they might search the Robbers Roost area first. Even then, the earliest

they'll reach me is Thursday. I'll try to stay alive as long as I can, but I can't imagine living longer than one more day. This means help will arrive too late. By Thursday, I'll be dead. And this video will be history.'

CHAPTER 8
The raven

70 hrs 45 mins

7.30 am That last video recording was the most pessimistic so far. It's strange, but the feeling of hopelessness doesn't last. As the sky grows brighter, I think of the raven. The bird is a sign of hope. Just thinking about it makes me want to do something.

I try lifting the boulder once more. I make the rope even shorter, but when I step on it, nothing happens. I do everything I can to make it work. I push, jump and shout as I put all my weight onto the rope. It's still no good. The boulder doesn't move a millimetre.

I step down and lay my head on the boulder. I feel like crying but I can't. There's not enough water in my body to produce any tears. But there's still the knife. It's lying open on top of the boulder.

Suddenly, I know what I'm going to do. Quickly, I put the tourniquet around my arm and tighten it. Then I pick up the multi-tool, open the shorter knife and push it hard into my arm. This time, the knife goes all the way in.

I pull out the knife and look at the deep hole I've made in my right arm. I can't believe I've done this. It didn't even hurt and there's very little blood. I can see the bones in my arm through the hole. I will never be able to cut through them with only a small knife.

It's time for a drink. I pick up the bottle and feel the last of the water disappear down my throat. I check the time. It's exactly 8.00 am and all I have to drink now is urine.

71 hrs 45 mins

8.30 am The raven appears. It's fifteen minutes late but I'm happy. I was beginning to think it wouldn't come. I feel happy and start thinking of all the wonderful times I've spent with friends and family. I remember a trip to Washington D.C. with my sister, and another to Gettysburg with my dad. I also think of all the adventures I've had with different friends. The time passes quickly. Midday arrives without me realising.

I urinate into the CamelBak. Then I pour the clearer half of the urine into my water bottle. I throw the rest away. I have no idea how long anyone can survive on urine alone. At least drinking it wasn't as bad as I expected.

It is now the warmest part of the day. This is the time I am most comfortable. I have found the best way to sit and feel calmer in the warm air. Perhaps help will arrive in time. If so, I will soon be as free as the raven.

Three hours later, I have reached the end of my third day trapped in the canyon. None of my plans of escape have worked. All I can do is stay strong for another night and hope for rescue.

I eat the last burrito. It is too dry to get down my throat so I take a mouthful of urine. The urine tastes better at night because it's colder, but it's still going to be a long, hard night.

* * *

On Wednesday morning, Brion After was at work in the shop. At nine-fifteen he called Leona to check if he had arrived, but he hadn't. Brion had waited long enough. He picked up the phone. Aron's mother answered on the first ring.

'Mrs Ralston?'

'Yes?'

'This is Brion After – Aron's boss at Ute Mountaineer. I'm afraid I'm rather worried about him. He hasn't returned from a trip he took last week. Do you know where he went? No one here has seen him since last Wednesday.'

'Oh dear,' said Aron's mother. 'I have no idea where he is. I called him last week and left a message, but he didn't call back. Did he tell any of his housemates where he was going?'

'No, just that he might hike somewhere in the Canyonlands area of Utah,' explained Brion

'I think you should call the Aspen police.'

'Yes, I'll do that right now. I'll let you know what happens.'

'Thank you, Brion.'

Mrs Ralston's hand was shaking as she put down the phone. She suddenly had an idea. Perhaps Aron had sent an email to one of his friends saying where he was going? She went to the computer. Aron had an email address – but what was it? She found his name, but had to answer a secret question to read his emails. None of the answers she gave worked but she kept trying. In the end, she guessed the correct answer and sent the information to Brion.

After Brion had called the Aspen police, the head officer, Adam Crider, started the rescue operation. He called Mrs Ralston for the license-plate number of her son's truck. Mrs Ralston had written it down on a piece of paper. When she read it to Officer Crider, she didn't realise it was wrong. Aron had given it to her in a hurry and made a mistake.

Officer Crider called back and told Mrs Ralston there was

no record of that license-plate. This left her with another problem. How could she find the correct license-plate number?

Brion After was having better luck. He had found a list of email addresses for Aron's climbing friends. Perhaps they knew where he was. He wanted to check immediately, but he had to leave for Australia that day. He called Aron's housemate Elliot and asked him to manage the store and rescue operation until he returned. Elliot agreed.

When Elliot reached the store, he received a call from Mrs Ralston. She wanted to check the license-plate number she had given Brion. It was on his desk. Elliot checked as she read out the number.

'Wait. Did you say 886, Mrs Ralston?'

'Yes.'

'Brion made a mistake. He wrote down 888. I'll call Officer Crider and give him the correct number.'

By early afternoon, Elliot had received an email from Steve Pratchett, the most important of Aron's climbing friends. Steve had climbed for many years. He often led rescue operations to find climbers lost in the mountains. Another friend, Jason, had sent Steve a list of all the canyons Aron said he wanted to hike in Canyonlands. Steve called the Utah police for the area and spoke to one the main officers, Kyle Ekker. Officer Ekker was very helpful. Steve gave him the latest license-plate number for Aron's truck and Officer Ekker sent his men out to look for it.

They returned as night fell. There was no sign of the truck. Officer Ekker checked the number with the national license office. There was no vehicle on record. Once again, the number was wrong.

The bad news reached Aron's mother. Then she remembered that Aron was living in Albuquerque, New Mexico, when he bought the truck. The vehicle license office for the area was in Santa Fe. She called and an officer searched the records and found Aron's name. The records showed his license-plate number as NM 846-MMY.

Finally, they had the correct number. The information was given to Officer Ekker. It was too late to continue searching that night. It would have to wait until the morning.

'Wait for us, Aron,' Mrs Ralston said as she went to bed. 'We're coming.'

* * *

89 hrs 15 mins

2.00 am The darkness seems unreal. In fact, I don't know what is real and what isn't anymore. I start to have visions. Friends suddenly appear in the canyon like silent ghosts and wave me towards them. I follow and find myself in some place I know from the past. They smile at me in a kind way, but they never speak. Because of their kindness, I am not afraid. I know they are protecting me. I am happy while the visions last. To me,

they are real. It is only when they disappear and the cold and pain return that I know they are not. Then, shaking hard, I continue chipping at the boulder. After that, I sit again and it's not long before the visions return. During the second half of the night, I have visions of myself as a child. Sometimes I'm playing cards with my grandfather. Other times I am running across bright green fields with my friends.

Something about the visions tells me that I have not given the people I care about enough attention. I'm always thinking of the things I want to achieve and not noticing other people. Now I realise that my love for friends and family is the main reason I want to escape. The thought of seeing them again is keeping me alive. I promise myself that if I can escape from here back to the people, I will be kinder towards them.

The visions always include some kind of drink. It is usually something cold and sweet like apple juice or ice tea. Just as I am about to drink, the vision disappears and I wake up. Then I feel the cold and the pain of the rope against my legs. I stand up and begin my routine all over again.

However, the visions tell me something: I am not ready to die. As morning comes on the fifth day, I feel sure I can still last a few more days. I don't know if this is true, but I'm still alive when the sun rises. The raven appears on time. The sound of its wings and the light in the canyon are beautiful. I watch its smooth flight, following the line of the canyon. I take out my camera and film as it disappears from view.

CHAPTER 9
'It's his truck'

97 hrs 45 mins

10.30 am I don't want to look at my watch. When I did this last night the time seemed to pass more slowly. I have a new idea. It came to me as I was looking at all the rocks around me. Why not find a hard rock and use it to break the boulder? There's one in a hole in the canyon wall above me. It is round and black. I reach up and pull it out. It's perfect – just the right size and weight.

I hit the rock hard against the boulder. Little bits of stone fly into the air. It's working. I continue, but soon have to stop because of the pain in my left hand. I decide to rest for a while.

Early afternoon is usually the warmest time of day. But today it's only thirteen degrees, the coldest day so far. It also means that tonight will be the coldest night. Realising this makes me want to do something while it's still light.

The problem with using the black rock was that it hurt my left hand. But what if I tie a sock around my hand to protect it? I do this and it works. By 6.00 pm I have taken off more of the boulder in three hours than I did in four days. But it's still not enough. And even with the sock there is too much pain in my left hand to continue.

I put down the rock. I feel sure I won't survive another night in the canyon. I finally accept this. There is nothing else I can do to save myself.

110 hrs 15 mins

11.00 pm The canyon feels as cold as ice. I have been awake for over a hundred hours. Another night of the sitting –

standing routine will kill me. I haven't had any clean water since eight o'clock yesterday morning, only urine. How much longer can I survive? Death could come at any moment. I am so certain of this that I take the knife and write the dates of my life on the canyon wall. When I have finished I read them by the light of my headlamp: ARON OCT 75 - APR 03.

Around midnight, I have another vision. I am walking alone through the canyon wall. On the other side is a living room. I step inside and look around. A little boy in a red shirt comes into the room. I guess he must be about three. Suddenly, I know who he is. He is my future son and the room is in my future home. The little boy runs across the wooden floor, laughing. I pick him up with my left arm. My right arm has no hand. Then I put him onto my shoulder and he laughs even more. He holds my arms in his little hands and together we dance around the room. The sun is shining and I feel free, happy, and alive.

The vision disappears. I am back in the canyon again, but now I don't feel the same as before. Seeing the boy has changed everything. Now, even with the cold, pain, tiredness and thirst, I am sure I will survive.

* * *

On Thursday, May the 1st, Kyle Ekker was looking at a map of the Canyonlands area on his office wall. The clock above read 9.07 am. Already that morning, his men had searched the top and centre of the area and found nothing.

What about the Robbers Roost canyons in the south? The only roads down there were made of rocks and sand. It might take longer to search. He called Glen Sherrill, the head officer for the area. When Glen answered the phone Kyle described Aron's truck.

'It's a red Toyota. License number NM 846-MMY.'

'I think I've seen a truck like that,' Glen replied. 'I'll radio one of my men and ask them to check.'

Kyle thanked him and put down the phone.

Twenty minutes later, Glen called back. 'Officer Kyle?'

'Speaking.'

'Glen Sherrill here. We've found the truck you're looking for. It's in the Horseshoe Canyon carpark.'

By 10.00 am the good news had reached Elliot, Steve, and Mrs Ralston. Steve immediately arranged for a rescue team to join the police and help in the search. Half an hour later, they were on their way. Things were now moving fast.

CHAPTER 10
Escape

120 hrs

8.45 am It's Thursday, May the 1st. 120 hours without sleep. Two days without water. I can't believe I'm still alive. I didn't think I'd survive beyond Wednesday. Perhaps the vision of the little boy kept me alive last night. But now, with no sign of a rescue, my hopes are disappearing fast.

I am also upset because the raven hasn't appeared. It's never been this late before. I try and forget about the bird and pick up the camcorder. I am certain that this will be my last message to my family.

I am calm as I leave necessary instructions for my parents. I tell them to give most of my things to Sonja. Then I tell them what to do with my dead body. The video ends with three simple words: 'I love you.'

I'm crying as I close the camcorder for the last time. But there are no tears – my body is too dry for tears.

Now I can only wait. I can't accept this. I've discovered that nothing I can do will help me escape. But it's better to be doing something than nothing. I pick up the black rock and hit it as hard as I can against the boulder. I continue, trying to forget the pain in my left hand. In the end, I can't. I try to drop the rock, but the fingers of my hand won't open.

What have you done now? asks the first voice.

Stay calm, says the second.

Slowly, my fingers loosen and the stone falls out of my hand. I look at my other arm. It's covered with bits of rock. As I'm removing these with the knife I push too hard and the blade goes through the skin near my wrist. I don't feel anything. That part of my arm must be dead. My right hand died long ago. It's now a dark blue colour. I push the knife through the skin of my thumb. There's a sound as some gas escapes, followed by a bad smell.

The arm is poisoned and the poison will kill me. I don't want the arm to be a part of me anymore. I throw myself against the boulder. When I look at my arm, I see that it's in a strange position.

That moment is like the sun coming out. I realise what it means. I can break my arm by using my own weight. That means I won't have to cut through bone anymore. I throw the whole weight of my body below the boulder. There is a loud noise. I keep going. There is a second loud noise. I've done it! I've broken both bones in my arm.

I tie the tourniquet, take the knife and begin cutting. The only thing on my mind is escape, but the pain is terrible. I scream as I push down with the knife.

For almost one hour the pain, screams, and cutting continue.

122 hrs 47 mins

11.32 am Finally, I feel the knife hit rock on the other side of my arm. I fall back with a single thought screaming through my head.

You've done it, Aron! You're FREE! FREE! FREE!

There's no time to lose. Blood is coming out of the end of my arm and it's a long walk back to my truck.

I tighten the tourniquet. Then I tie my climbing bag

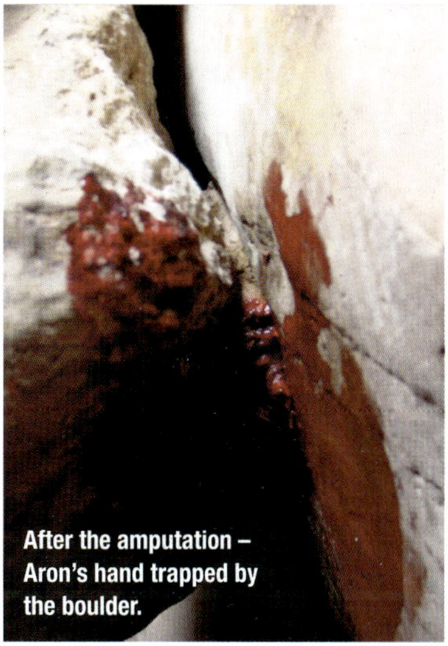

After the amputation – Aron's hand trapped by the boulder.

on my arm to hold it. I tighten it around my neck and put my things inside. Before I leave, I take two pictures of the part of my arm still trapped by the boulder. Now I am ready to go.

I can't walk straight. My body crashes from one side of the canyon wall to the other. I stop. My heart is going much too fast. I could still die at any moment. I make myself stay calm. What I need most of all is water. There might be some at the Big Drop Rappel, but first I need to get there.

It takes me twenty minutes. I stand at the edge and look down. It is just over eighteen metres to the canyon floor.

At the bottom of Big Drop Rappel. Aron rappelled down with only one arm.

There are metal rings in the rock for climbers. I tie my rope to them and rappel down*. With only one arm, this is

* See Canyons and canyoning, page 6.

not easy. For once I am careful as I go down the rope. I reach the bottom and turn. On the ground in front of me is a pool of brown water. It's full of dead mosquitoes but I don't care. I fill my bottle and drink one litre in a few seconds. I drink another and don't want to move. I just want to stay there for the rest of my life.

That won't be long if you don't start walking. There are still twelve kilometres to go.

The voice is right. I drink one more litre, slowly this time. Then I fill my bottle and the CamelBak and begin walking. Blood is coming out faster from my arm now. I wonder if I can get back to the truck in time.

Things start to go wrong. I get lost up a side canyon and have to turn round. Then I notice that water is coming out of my CamelBak. There's a hole in it. Quickly, I drink the rest of the water. Now I only have the water in the water bottle. This has to last all the way back to the truck and the temperature is rising. I am so weak and tired I can't imagine surviving that long. I take a sip and keep the water in my mouth as I walk. That seems to help.

I still wonder if I can get back to my truck. I can't walk straight, I can't think for more than a few seconds, and I'm losing blood, fast.

125 hrs 10 mins

1.55 pm I've arrived at the Great Gallery. The paintings are amazing but all I can think of is water. There is more here. I stop to fill the water bottle. It has taken me two and a half hours to travel six kilometres. For someone close to death I have done well. But my problems are getting worse every minute. Blood is now coming from my arm really fast and I'm in terrible pain from the amputation. I want to stop and rest, but I can't. I must go on.

I walk as fast as I can. By two-thirty I have covered nearly ten kilometres. Only three more kilometres to my truck, but I'm feeling weaker every minute.

125 hrs 45 mins

2.30 pm I've come to another huge canyon. The walls must be over thirty metres high. Ahead of me is a steep hill. This is bad news. I'll never be able to climb it – I'm too weak. Something makes me look again. I shake my head, unable to believe what I see.

About seventy metres ahead of me are a family of three people – a man, a woman and a young boy. They are walking away from me.

'HELP! HELP! PLEASE! I NEED HELP! '

They turn and come running towards me.

When they reach me, I begin telling my story: 'My name is Aron Ralston. I was trapped by a boulder in the canyon for five days. This morning, I had to amputate my arm to escape. I need a doctor. I'm losing blood, fast .... ' Unable to continue, I fall to the ground.

The man gives me a bottle of water. 'The police at the carpark told us about you,' he says.

His name is Eric. His wife is Monique and his son is called Andy. They are tourists from the Netherlands. Eric gives me more water while Monique and Andy run back to get the police. After about ten minutes, Eric helps me up and we continue walking slowly.

The steep trail is ahead. Even with Eric's help, I know I won't be able to climb it. 'How will I ever get out of here?' I ask myself.

CHAPTER 11
127 hours

126 hrs 18 mins

3.03 pm A noise somewhere above me answers the question. It's a helicopter! A helicopter to take me to hospital. I can't believe it! It doesn't seem real. I sit down and wait as a man jumps to the ground and walks towards me.

'Are you Aron Ralston?' he asks.

'Yes.'

A second man gets out of the helicopter and they help me inside. I ask one of the men to get my climbing bag. Eric gives it to him.

'Thank you, Eric,' I say. 'Thanks for everything.' I wave goodbye as the helicopter rises into the air.

I sit behind the pilot and watch blood pour slowly down my arm.

Be strong, Aron. You're almost safe.

'Keep him talking,' the pilot says to his partner.

'Where are we going?' I ask the second man.

'We're taking you to the hospital in Moab,' he replies.

'How long will that take?'

'It's about twelve minutes from here.'

He asks me what happened in the canyon and I begin telling my story. By the time I finish, we are circling around Moab. I look down and see an area of green grass below. This gets bigger as we move down towards it. I realise we are landing in front of the hospital. A man who looks like a policeman is standing with two nurses in white coats on the hospital steps. The helicopter lands and the nurses carry me into the building.

They put me in an empty room. The man walks in and introduces himself. 'Hi, Aron. I'm Steve, and I'm a Park Ranger*.'

As the nurses take off my shoes, I ask Steve to let my mother know that I'm OK and to arrange for someone to collect all the things I left at Horseshoe Canyon.

'I'll do that when we've finished here,' Steve replies.

He wants to know what happened in the canyon. Once again, I tell my story. It's the third time I've done this in two hours. When I finish, I can see that Steve wants to ask me a lot of questions.

He doesn't get the chance. A doctor comes back into the room with a large needle.

'Wait!' I say as she goes to put it into my skin. 'I have a problem with needles. I sometimes go into shock. I fell out of a chair once.'

The doctor looks surprised. 'You mean you're not in shock already?'

*A Park Ranger works in a national park, looking after it and helping in rescues.

'I don't know,' I reply.

'Look, do you want this for the pain or not?'

'Damn it, yes!' I say. I continue talking to Steve as the needle goes into my arm.

127 hrs

3.45 pm I suddenly hear another man's voice. He sounds like a doctor. He pulls at the things over my right arm and asks Steve what they are.

'There are a couple of tourniquets under there,' Steve replies.

'No, just one,' I whisper. I look at the clock on the wall. It's 3.45 pm on Thursday, May the 1st. I realise that my nightmare has lasted for exactly 127 hours. It's my last thought before falling into a long, deep sleep.

EPILOGUE

My rescue was only the first part of a long, difficult fight back to health. In that first month, I had five operations. I was also taking eighteen different medicines a day. Most were for the pain and to fight the poison in my blood. While I was taking them, I couldn't do anything well. I couldn't sleep and my thoughts were unclear. After ten days in hospital, I went home. A week later, I was back in hospital in Denver for my fifth and most difficult operation. The time I woke up after the operation was the lowest point after my escape. I felt terrible. I couldn't eat, I couldn't sleep and I was still in pain. Later, I discovered that I nearly died. However by May the 25th, I was home to stay.

The following weeks were difficult for my family. I was like a child again, unable to do anything for myself. Slowly, however, things got better. I was soon eating normal food and by the end of the summer I was the same weight as before the accident.

By this time, I had a prosthetic arm. I learnt to use it quite well. I felt pleased. It wouldn't be long before I would be able

Climbing the North Face of North Maroon Peak, May 2004.

to go climbing again. Of course, I didn't tell my mother that.

On August the 31st, four months after the accident, I spoke at Sonja's wedding. Four days later, I climbed Mount Moran in Wyoming with eight of my friends.

On October the 25th – two days before my twenty-eighth birthday – I returned to Blue John Canyon. Some friends, including Kristi Moore, were with me. We filmed the place where the accident happened. Then, as the others made their way back to their vehicles, I stayed behind for a few minutes. Just before I left, I looked at the dates of my life on the canyon wall. I was wrong. My life didn't end in the canyon. Thoughts of the people I love had kept me alive. If I wanted to see them again, I had to survive. That's what I told myself. And that's what I did.

My accident changed my life. I know that even if I could travel back in time, I wouldn't change anything. I would still say goodbye to Megan and Kristi and continue alone. I've learned a lot from that choice. I believe we are on Earth to do the things we love, even if that means making a hard choice. Sometimes, that means cutting out something and leaving it in the past. Saying goodbye to things from our past is also a new beginning.

Making *127 Hours*

'*127 Hours* is an action film with a guy who can't move,' says Danny Boyle, the director of the film. It sounds an impossible subject, but *127 Hours* was one of the most successful films of 2011. So how did Danny Boyle do it and why did he want to make this film?

'I have to make this film'

It all started with a book called *Between a rock and a hard place*. This was Aron Ralston's book about the time he spent trapped in the canyon in Utah. When Danny read the book, he knew that he had to make the film. Aron's nightmare finally ended after 127 hours, so Danny chose *127 Hours* as the title.

Different views

When Danny met Aron for the first time in 2006, he told him he wanted to make a drama film of his story using only one main actor. But Aron wanted the film to be a documentary. It had to be true. For three years, neither man could agree. Then Danny won an Oscar for his film *Slumdog Millionaire*. After this success, Aron agreed that Danny should make the film his way. The result is an amazing biographical adventure film. Of course, Danny included some scenes in the film that didn't happen in real life, but they add to the drama of the film. For example, there is a scene where Aron, Megan and Kristi go swimming, and another where Aron interviews himself with the camcorder.

Have you seen any other films of true stories where someone had to fight to survive? Talk about them with your class.

James Franco and Danny Boyle talk on the set of *127 Hours.*

Filming in Blue John Canyon

Finding the right actor was very difficult, but as soon as he met James Franco, Danny was sure he could play Aron's part just right.

When everything was ready, Boyle and Franco spent a week filming in Blue John Canyon. However, they decided that filming the trapped arm in the canyon was too dangerous, so a special set was built. For the amputation, Danny used two false arms with plastic bones. This made the amputation look and sound very real. It was so real that several people fainted when they watched that scene in cinemas.

What do these words mean? You can use a dictionary.

biographical drama documentary scene interview set faint

Utah, a land of parks and

If you love outdoor adventure, Utah is one of the best US states to visit. Every year, over a million tourists explore its five National Parks. Canyonlands, where Aron Ralston went, is the biggest. Here, the most popular activities are hiking, mountain-biking, horse-riding, rock-climbing and canyoning.

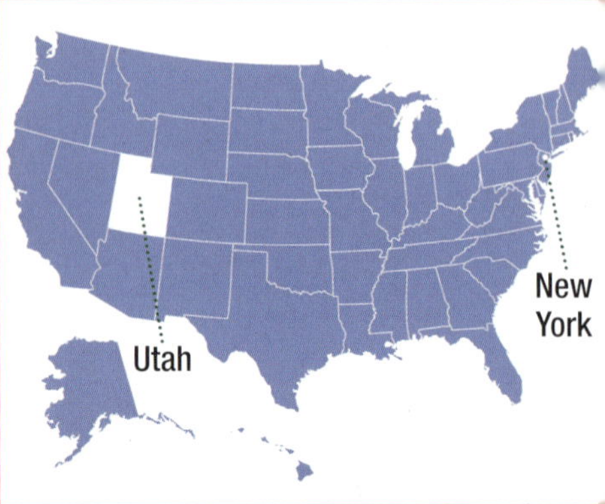

The Great Gallery

A hike of around five kilometres into Horseshoe Canyon takes visitors to a place called the Great Gallery. The rock paintings on its walls are between two and eight thousand years old. The tallest is over two metres high. It's known as 'The Great Ghost' because of its size and strange appearance. Who painted it? What does it mean? No one knows.

What national parks are there in your country? What activities can you do in them? Are any of the activities dangerous?

Biking and climbing

The White Rim Trail in Canyonlands is over 160 kilometres long. It takes three to four days to bike it, but it's worth it for the fantastic views.

Taylor Canyon is the most popular place in the park for rock-climbers. Its sandstone towers are one of the few areas in the park where the rock is not too soft to climb.

Canyoning

A dangerous sport

Only people who have done a lot of climbing should try canyoning, or 'canyoneering' as it's called in America. It's easy to get trapped or lost and when there's no water the dry heat can kill a person in as little as two days. Too much water is also dangerous. If there is a sudden storm, water quickly fills the canyons. People drown every year because of this. The climbing is difficult, too. Canyon walls can be slippery, soft rock can break at any time, and boulders can fall without warning.

What do these words mean? You can use a dictionary.

outdoor **sandstone tower** **drown** **slippery** **waterfall**

Through land and water

Canyoning is not only a dry land activity. In many parts of the world, canyoners travel through rivers, streams, waterfalls and even over ice. This can be very exciting, but you need special equipment for these trips.

Utah has some of the best dry land canyons in the world. For canyoning through water, Chitwan National Park in Nepal has everything from fast rivers and streams to huge waterfalls. One of the most popular places for ice-canyoning is Monte Sainte Anne near Quebec, in Canada.

Remember!

If you decide to go hiking or climbing, safety is very important.

- Always go with a friend, never alone.
- Always tell people where you are going.
- Take plenty of food and water.
- Check the weather before you go.
- If you have an accident, light a fire at night. Rescue planes fly at night and a fire can help them find you.

'Anything is possible':

Aron Ralston lost his right arm, but three months later he was climbing mountains again. Like Aron, there are many people in the world of sport who have achieved fantastic things even with a disability. Read these three amazing stories.

Oscar Pistorius 'The fastest man on no legs'

Oscar Pistorius, the South African runner, was born without bones in both legs. Doctors had to amputate both his lower legs when he was only eleven months old. This disability didn't stop Oscar. He got special prosthetic legs and became a successful sports player and won medals in several team sports at school. In 2003, he decided to become a runner. He did so well at the Paralympic Games (the Olympic Games for athletes with disabilities) that he became known as 'the fastest man on no legs'.

But Oscar dreamed of competing against athletes without disabilities. He had to fight the sports authorities, but finally they let him. In July 2011, Oscar won a 400m race in Italy! He described this as his biggest success. His dream is to win gold at the Olympic Games. 'I've never felt sorry for myself,' Oscar says. 'I just enjoy what I do and do it as well as I can.'

What do these words mean?
You can use a dictionary.
disability medal compete athlete authorities shark raise

Do you know other people with disabilities who have achieved amazing things? Talk to a partner.

disability and sport

'I love it too much to stop' Bethany Hamilton

When she was only thirteen, surfer Bethany Hamilton lost her left arm in a shark attack off the coast of Hawaii. Many people thought that she would never surf again. But although she nearly died in the attack, just one month later Bethany was back in the water. It wasn't easy learning to surf with only one arm. 'The hardest thing was just learning how to stand up and position yourself in the right place,' she says.

Two years later, Bethany came first in the National Championships, a top surfing competition. Like Aron, Bethany, says other people helped with her success.

'Anything is possible' Rick Hansen

By the age of fifteen, Canadian Rick Hansen was winning competitions in five different sports. Then he had a serious car accident and had to use a wheelchair. But Rick didn't allow this to end his dream of becoming a top athlete. After years of hard training, he was accepted onto the Canadian Paralympic Team and won three gold and two silver medals in the games of 1980 and 1984.

Winning wasn't enough for Rick – he wanted to help others too. In March 1985, he began his 'Man In Motion World Tour'.

He travelled through 34 countries in 26 months, through all types of weather, in his wheelchair. When Rick returned to Canada he had raised more than 26 million dollars to help athletes with disabilities!

'What was the most difficult part of the tour?' people asked.

'Starting,' said Rick. 'I couldn't have done it without the help of other people.'

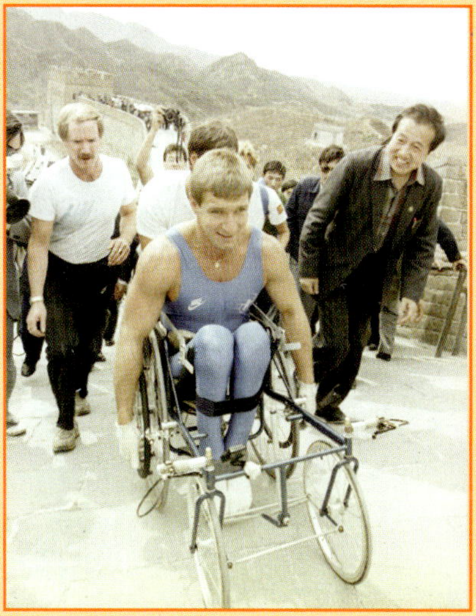

PROLOGUE – CHAPTER 4

Before you read

You can use a dictionary for this section

1 Choose the correct word.

- a) The path was very flat, but it was a long **climb / hike**.
- b) The **road / trail** through the forest was only wide enough for one person.
- c) A **mountain / boulder** is a big rock that can move.
- d) Pete and Sam share a flat together. They are **workers / housemates**.
- e) Drinking slowly is better for you. You should **sip / shoot** your water.

2 Complete the sentences with these words:

drop trapped shock chip amputate shake bike routine

- a) After the accident, he couldn't move his leg because it was . . . . under a car. In the end, doctors had to . . . . his leg to free him. They cut it off below the knee.
- b) I decided to . . . . to school because I wanted some exercise.
- c) I climbed down the canyon. The rope didn't reach all the way down so I had to . . . . to the ground.
- d) 'I can't keep my hands still. They always . . . . like this when it's cold.'
- e) This knife isn't very sharp. I can only . . . . this stick a little at a time.
- f) I get up at seven o'clock every morning. This has become a . . . .
- g) They told me the president had died suddenly. I couldn't believe it. It was a . . . .

3 Look at the map of the Big Drop Rappel on page 5. Do you think it will be easy to get to the water pool? Look at pages 6 and 7 – what equipment and techniques will Aron need to use, do you think?

After you read

4 Are these sentences true or false?

- a) The words of the first voice always help Aron.
- b) Aron told his friends exactly where he was going on his trip.
- c) In the picture on page 12, Megan is the girl on the right.

d) Aron only has two litres of water and no food with him.
e) The boulder traps Aron's left hand against the canyon wall.
f) Aron thinks of three ways of escaping from the boulder.
g) Aron thinks he will only be able to survive for four days.
h) Kristi and Megan slept in Little Wild Horse Canyon.
i) Aron stops chipping because his left arm hurts.

5 What do you think?
Aron thinks that no one will miss him before Tuesday morning. Why does he think this? Do you think he is right?

CHAPTERS 5 – 8

Before you read

6 Complete the sentences with these words:
raven tourniquet mosquitoes last urinate bone license-plate visions

a) The nurse tied a piece of rubber around the patient's arm as a . . . to stop the blood.
b) I fell over this morning and now I can't walk. I think I've broken a . . . .
c) I drank three litres of water this morning. A little later I needed to . . . .
d) The . . . is a very large black bird.
e) There were large red spots on my skin. . . . had bitten me.
f) ARJ 279 is the number of the . . . of my car.
g) The doctor told him that the pictures in his head weren't real. They were only . . . .
h) There is a lot of food. It will . . . a long time.

7 What do you think will happen when Aron doesn't arrive for work on Tuesday morning?

After you read

8 Who says these things?
a) 'Help! Help!'
b) 'I'll be upset if he doesn't come.'
c) 'I think something might be wrong.'
d) 'I think you should call the Aspen police.'
e) 'I'll call Officer Crider and give him the correct number.'
f) 'Wait for us, Aron. We're coming.'

9 What do you think?

a) Why does the sight of the raven make Aron feel more hopeful?

b) Why does Aron make a second video recording to his family?

c) Why is Aron not afraid of the people he sees in his visions?

CHAPTERS 9 – EPILOGUE

Before you read.

10 Complete the sentences with these words:

prosthetic poison needle operation helicopter

a) If something dirty gets into your blood it can ... it.

b) His real arm was amputated. Now he has a ... arm.

c) 'Ow! That feels sharp,' he said as the ... went into his skin.

d) I felt the wind on my face as the ... landed on the ground.

e) The doctors gave her a new heart, but it was a long difficult ...

After you read

11 Answer the questions.

a) When was Aron's truck found?

b) Does Aron have to cut through his bones to amputate his arm?

c) Is it easy for Aron to rappel down the Big Drop?

d) Who are Eric, Monique and Andy? How do they help Aron?

e) How does Aron get to the hospital in Moab?

f) How many times does Aron tell his story? Who to?

g) How long was Aron in hospital? Did he get better quickly? How do you know?

12 What do you think?

At the end of the book, Aron says, 'The accident changed my life'. In what ways do you think Aron's life has changed after the accident? Make a list comparing the kind of person he was before the accident and the person he became after he was rescued.